James Downey

Why?
By James Downey

Copyright © 2018

Unless otherwise indicated, Scripture taken from the HOLY BIBLE, NEW INTERNATIONAL VERSION®. NIV®. Copyright © 1973, 1978, 1984 by International Bible Society. Used by permission of Zondervan. All rights reserved worldwide.

Scripture quotations marked (NLT) are taken from the Holy Bible, New Living Translation, copyright ©1996, 2004, 2015 by Tyndale House Foundation. Used by permission of Tyndale House Publishers, Inc., Carol Stream, Illinois 60188. All rights reserved.

Scripture quotations identified KJV are taken from the Holy Bible, King James Version, Cambridge, 1769.

Published by: New Freedom Books
Email: j.d.vrod@gmail.com

FOREWORD

Playing to a challenging audience can be tough. I was
a little nervous as I stood before a group of teenagers
incarcerated at the County detention center, ready
to present a church service together with another
volunteer who had been doing this for some time. A
couple of months prior, I sat mostly as an observer,
as the other volunteer tried to weave Biblical events
into an explanation of life that would resonate with
skeptical, struggling, and troubled youth. I launched
into my own version, incorporating a few different
angles but fell short of what I had hoped to
accomplish. Still, I noticed that some of what we
were doing registered with the teens. Maybe, I
thought, there is an interpretation of life that makes
sense to anyone who wonders why humanity is
forever trapped in a chaotic, combative state from
which we can't seem to escape. Adults are just as
skeptical, struggling and troubled as teenagers. We

are haunted by the question of why the world is so screwed up if there is a God who loves us. Can the answer be found in the Bible? Even if you don't believe in God or the Bible, why reject the possibility that our answers lie there without giving the idea a chance?

In order to answer such questions as why bad things happen to good people or why hundreds or thousands continue to die from disease, natural disasters, wars, terrorism, and senseless shootings, we need to understand God's original plan for mankind and how one bad choice, long, long ago by one man, rejected that plan, gave evil a foothold in the world, and brought condemnation upon mankind. We need to know our story from the time we were created to the end of time. We need to know the attributes of God and how he has provided mankind the way back to him to fulfill God's original plan. The history of the Bible, mankind's journey since creation, and the saga of the nation of Israel, all help our understanding.

Table of Contents

Why the Bible?

Many people question whether God exists. As we look around, it's not hard to see why. Like a true-or-false quiz, we have a 50-50 chance to get the right answer. He exists or he doesn't. Likewise, many people question whether the Bible is the word of God. Several books claim to be the only true source of God's word, and they contradict one another. For example, the Koran strongly contradicts many of the most important principles of the Bible. Likewise, The Book of Mormon and the version of the Bible followed by Jehovah's Witnesses vary in significant respects from the Christian Bible.

Biblical Christianity is based upon God reaching down to mankind. In contrast, other religions are based upon mankind trying to reach up to God, usually through man's own works. In religions that hold, contrary to the Bible, that God is reached through good deeds, there is no sure way to know how many and what kinds of good deeds are needed to get into Heaven. Nor is there any sure way to know how many or what kinds of bad deeds will erase good deeds.

The Bible is not one book written by one author at one sitting. It is a collection of sixty-six books written over about 1,500 years by some forty authors. Those who believe in it can point to many factors that support its accuracy. For example, there are some three hundred prophecies (foretelling future events) made in the Old Testament, which have already been fulfilled. The odds of this happening without God's hand are essentially zero. The Bible is considered to be inspired by God, inerrant, and complete—in contrast to other theological writings. The independent historical verifications of the Bible far surpass those of other religious writings, as well as most other historical works.

The Bible encompasses the entire time period from the creation of the universe to a future end time when the earth will be shattered by a cataclysmic war centered in the Middle East between forces of good and evil that will destroy much of mankind. The Bible is divided into the Old

Testament and the New Testament. The Old Testament traces the period from the beginning of creation to a time about four hundred years before the birth of Jesus Christ, a little over two thousand years ago. The New Testament traces the time and events from the birth of Jesus to approximately one hundred years after his death. Revelation, the last chapter of the Bible, describes the end times of the earth as we know it and the final war between good and evil, which will center on Jerusalem at an unknown future time. Some think we are close to that time.

For our purpose, we start with two premises: God exists, and the Bible is his inspired word. There is a monumental body of evidence that the Bible is divinely inspired by God, but what people wish to believe is ultimately their choice. For the time being, anyone skeptical as to either premise should at least benefit from believing they are *possibly* true. If we take the time to study the issue and examine the various holy books and religions with an open mind—rather than simply accepting popular notions, soothing and comfortable ideas, or misguided teachings in school and the media—we can reach an informed decision. Study, compare, and contrast the Bible, the Koran, the Book of Mormon, and other such literature. Search out their historical contexts and proofs of their reliability and veracity. An accurate view of God is vital, not only to our understanding of who and where we are but also to our very existence. Isn't this worth an investment of our time?

The cultural controversy doesn't give the Bible a chance to get out of the starting gate. The first words of the first chapter of the Bible state:

> *In the beginning, God created the heavens and the earth.* — *Genesis 1:1*

Not so, say the evolutionists as well as the teachings of most public schools and universities.

Supposedly, all living things evolved from a single cell that came into being through chance.

If this is true:

- Our existence has no meaning or purpose. We are simply a cosmic accident.
- There is no standard of right or wrong except what we choose.
- We can change what is right and wrong at our whim to suit our own selfish desires.
- We are the ultimate powers.
- Death is like turning out a light.

- There are no eternal consequences to what we do during our lives. Get away with whatever we can; everybody does it. In other words, this seventy-to-eighty-year mortal life is as good as it gets.

If the Bible is true:

- There is a purpose and meaning to our lives.
- There is a much higher power in the universe than humans (and even alien superbeings from another planet).
- Physical death is not the end of our existence.
- There are eternal consequences to our choices and actions.
- There are standards of right and wrong higher than those we choose for ourselves.

So—are we the result of creation or evolution? Whichever view we choose will, consciously or subconsciously, govern our behavior and direct our life decisions. If you decide to study this issue further, seek out information on the concept of Intelligent Design, which at its core holds that the incredible complexity of life renders the theory of chance evolution proposed by Charles Darwin mathematically impossible.

As we observe peoples' behavior around us, which view seems to prevail today? To which do you subscribe?

What Is God Like?

In order to grasp the concept of creation by God, our mortal minds need to accomplish a seemingly impossible task: to comprehend a God who is beyond human comprehension. A.W. Tozer, in his book, *The Knowledge of the Holy*, explores the attributes of God found in the Bible. He opines that most of our problems come from an improper picture of God. The attributes Tozer identifies include these:

God is *omnipotent*. He has all power.

In the beginning, God created the heavens and the earth. — *Genesis 1:1*

Through him [the Word] all things were made; without him, nothing was made that has been made. — *John 1:3*

God is *sovereign*. He [not us] rules his entire creation.

> *The Most High is sovereign over all kingdoms on earth. — Daniel 4:25*

God is *omnipresent*. He surrounds creation. There is no place beyond him for anything to be. There is no place anywhere where we can hide from him. He knows our innermost thoughts (see Psalm 139).

God is *transcendent*. He exists outside of space and time. He is so far above human thought that we cannot conceive of him.

> *For my thoughts are not your thoughts, neither are your ways my ways. As the heavens are higher than the earth, so are my ways higher than your ways, and my thoughts than your thoughts. — Isaiah 55:8, 9*

God is *omniscient*. He possesses all knowledge. He cannot be taught anything, and indeed could never have a "teacher."

> *Who can fathom the mind of the Lord, or instruct the Lord as his counselor? Whom did the Lord consult to enlighten him, and who taught him the right way? — Isaiah 40:13, 14.*

God is *infinite*. He is limitless, an impossible thing for a limited (human) mind to grasp. He cannot be measured, as measurements have limits.

> *Can you probe the limits of the Almighty? — Job 11:7*

> *I am the Alpha and the Omega, the first and the last, the beginning and the end. — Revelation 22:12*

God is *eternal*. God exists outside of time. He has no past or future. He has always existed and will always exist. He has no deadlines or time limits in which to accomplish his will. Our entire lives are enslaved by time: seconds, minutes, hours, days, years . . . until our mortal end. We cannot grasp the idea of eternity.

> *From everlasting to everlasting, you are God…a thousand years in your sight are like a day that has just gone by. — Psalms 90: 2, 4*

> *For God so loved the world that he gave his one and only son, that whoever believes in him shall not perish but have eternal life. John 3:16*

God is *self-sufficient*. All created living things have needs in order to survive—such as food, water, and air. God has no need for anything. Rather, he is the provider of the needs for all the things he created. In him the universe is sustained.

The Father has life in Himself. — John 5:26.

And in him all things hold together. — Colossians 1:17

God is *self-existent*. He has no origin. Only created things have an origin (and a creator). Our minds can't understand this, for everything in our world has some sort of origin.

He is before all things, and in him all things hold together. Colossians 1:17

Moses said to God, "Suppose I go to the Israelites and say to them, 'The God of your fathers has sent me to you,' and they ask me, 'What is his name?' Then what shall I tell them?" God said to Moses, "I am who I am." — Exodus 13–14

God *possesses all wisdom*. In our pride, we often think of ourselves as wise. Sometimes we think we know better than God and try to run our lives contrary to his counsel. As we consider the attributes of God we find in the Bible, is self-reliance a wise choice?

The fear of the Lord [awesome respect] is the beginning of wisdom. — Psalms 111:10

The foolishness of God is wiser than human wisdom.
— *1 Corinthians 1:25*

Just considering one of God's attributes should leave us in awe and wonder. But to consider and realize that God possesses *all* of them should leave us speechless. When we consider the awesome power of God described by the foregoing attributes, we can begin to accept that such a God is capable of creating the universe, our Earth, and everything in it.

The foregoing are not all of God's attributes. As Tozer notes, the Bible tells us he is also full of grace, mercy, justice, goodness, holiness, faithfulness, and love. When we think of God, we should picture him properly, taking into account all of his astonishing attributes. In particular, we should always remember God's holiness, which exists on a plane incomprehensibly higher than the greatest perfection we can imagine.

So how did we get to where are today? Let's start at the beginning of time and work forward to the present day. We cannot study the history of mankind without studying the history of the nation of Israel, the Jewish people. We won't understand our present circumstances without this knowledge. Do you wonder why Israel is always in the news? Although

Israel's story is long, it is remarkable. Stick with the story to find out. It will be worth your time.

In the Beginning

Genesis, the first book of the Bible, describes the process of creation by God, who has the attributes and power to create all things. It is important to study the process of creation described in the Bible to make a particular point. Before doing that, let's pause to consider the universe God created, the area where we live.

If we look at the moon, we rarely think about what would happen if it suddenly fell from the sky and smashed into Earth. Yet nothing is holding it up there. In fact nothing is holding up Earth or any of the planetary bodies. They balance and suspend one another in space through the interaction of gravitational and centrifugal forces. This description is certainly elementary. Scientists have derived formulae to calculate the attractive forces of planetary bodies based on their mass and can predict and measure the movements of, and attractive forces of, planetary bodies. But none of us, not even the most brilliant scientists, have been able to figure out where gravity comes from. Google "where does gravity come from" for an entertaining tour of the subject. Can we accept the possibility that gravity was created by God when he created the heavens and the earth? The rotational speed of Earth at the equator is 1,037 miles per hour, yet nobody standing there flies off into space. Imagine being on a merry-go-round spinning that fast. Could any of us hold on?

Next, study some of the images captured by the Hubble space telescope and read about the millions, or even billions, of light years the universe spans (heavens), and the unbelievable number and size of distant galaxies and stars. If Earth were the size of a golf ball, the second-largest star thus far discovered, *Canis Majoris*, placed next to our golf ball would have a diameter as tall as Mount Everest—29,000 feet. By contrast, our own sun next to our golf ball would have a diameter of fifteen feet.

The heavens declare the glory of God. — Psalm 19:1

Now, consider how infinitely small planet Earth is, compared to the universe, and how much more infinitely small we are in that comparison. Some say the universe was created millions or billions of years ago in a massive explosion called the "big bang." Really? Where did the stuff that went bang come from, and who or what made it go bang?

With that framework in mind, let's examine the chronological steps of creation set forth in Genesis.

> *[In the beginning] the earth that was formless and empty, darkness was over the surface of the deep, and the Spirit of God was hovering over the waters. – Genesis 1:2*

> *God said, "let there be light," and there was light. God saw that the light was good. God . . . separated the light from the darkness. – Genesis 1:3–4*

God created the sky, separating the waters upon the earth from the water above it.

> *God said, "Let there be a vault between the waters to separate water from water." So God made the vault and separated the water under the vault from the water above it. – Genesis 1:6–7*

> *God said, "Let the land produce vegetation: seed-bearing plants and trees on the land that bear fruit with seed in it, according to their various kinds." . . . And God saw that it was good. – Genesis 1:11–12*

God said, "Let there be lights in the vault of the sky to separate the day from the night, and let them serve as signs to mark sacred times, and days and years.". . . God made two great lights—the greater light to govern the day and the lesser light to govern the night. He also made the stars. . . . And God saw that it was good. — Genesis 14—18

God said, "Let the water teem with living creatures, and let birds fly above the earth across the vault of the sky.". . . And God saw that it was good. — Genesis 1:20—21

God said, "Let the land produce living creatures according to their kinds: the livestock, the creatures that move along the ground, and the wild animals, each according to its kind." And God saw that it was good. — Genesis 1:24—25

God said, "Let us make mankind in our image, in our likeness, so that they may rule over the fish in the sea and the birds in the sky, over the livestock and all the wild animals, and over all the creatures that move along the ground." God saw all that he had made, and it was very good. And there was evening, and there was morning the sixth day. — Genesis 1:26, 31

Creating mankind "in our image" means that every person has inherent worth and that people share some of the characteristics of God. How does this compare with, and contrast to, the idea that people are just the result of many chance occurrences? If we evolved from monkeys, how come there are still monkeys?

The Bible ascribes the creation process to a period of six "days." The use of the term *days* has created a storm of controversy and is often contrasted to various fossil records and carbon-dating of ancient artifacts, which by themselves seem to indicate processes enduring over millions of years. Those who wish to deny that the universe was created by God, as described in the Bible, rely upon carbon-dating of such artifacts as proof, to them, that there is no guiding hand to creation. Some who believe the Bible take the term "day" literally, and indeed God as described in the Bible has the power and ability to create the universe in six twenty-four-hour days. Others interpret the term "day" figuratively, to simply denote a period of time in which sequential steps were taken by God, leading up to the creation of life. Indeed, 2 Peter 3:8 reminds us that "with the Lord, a day is like a thousand years, and a thousand years are like a day." Time is relevant only to mankind. It poses no constraints upon God, since he exists outside of time.

There are two points to consider here: The first is to recognize that the foundation of faith in the Bible begins with accepting the creation account in Genesis. We can't cherry pick what we want to believe in the Bible and discard the rest. Belief is an all-or-nothing proposition. Secondly, the Bible tells us that people were not subjected to death before the fall of mankind in the Garden of Eden, a topic that we will take up shortly. Any attempted explanation of creation and/or evolution that includes life-death cycles for mankind prior to the fall in the garden clashes with the Biblical account and cannot be rationally commingled with it.

Adam and Eve

In Genesis 2, we read that after God created man, he created woman.

> *God had planted a garden in the east, in Eden; and there he put the man he had formed. The Lord God made all kinds of trees grow out of the ground—trees that were pleasing to the eye and good for food. In the middle of the garden were the tree of life and the tree of the knowledge of good and evil. . . . God took the man and put him in the Garden of Eden to work it and take care of it. And the Lord God commanded the man, "You are free to eat from any tree in the garden; but you must not eat from the tree of the knowledge of good and evil, for when you eat from it you will certainly die."— Genesis 2:8–9, 15–17*

God could have created Adam incapable of making bad choices, but instead, Adam was given free will to make good or bad choices. Has mankind wisely used its free will over the thousands of years of its existence?

God pronounced the results of each progressive step of his creation "good," and when the first two people were added as the pinnacle, he pronounced that all he had made was *very* good. At this point, we see no mention of death or evil as active participants in creation, although they did exist. All creation is very good. When Adam is later introduced to the garden, he is given everything he needs to flourish and live—with one simple rule: don't eat from that one tree.

After Adam's creation:

> God said, "It is not good for the man to be alone. I will make a helper suitable for him." — Genesis 2:18

God then created a wife for Adam, named Eve. The process of the creation of woman is noteworthy because it defines the relationship God intended for the man and woman to each other.

> God caused the man to fall into a deep sleep; and while he was sleeping, he took one of the man's ribs and then closed up the place with flesh. Then the Lord God made a woman from the rib. . . . That is why a man leaves his father and mother and is united to his wife,

and they become one flesh. Adam and his wife were both naked, and they felt no shame. — Genesis 2:21–22, 24–25

Genesis 2:19–20 describes a period when God brought the animals of Earth to the man, allowing the man to name them.

There was, then, some period of childlike innocence when Adam and Eve lived in the Garden of Eden with the presence of God. Evil and death existed, but they could not be introduced to poison God's very good creation and intimate relationship with mankind, not without Adam and Eve's disobedience to God's one and only command. At that early time, mankind had everything needed to thrive in peace eternally on Earth, in loving fellowship with God. Adam and Eve lived that way—for a time. This was the way God intended us to live. How would it feel to live in that kind of world today?

We do not know how long Adam and Eve lived in that innocent paradise before creation was ruined, but Genesis later tells us that they, and by extension all of humanity born after them, could have lived in such circumstances forever—had they simply obeyed God. At that stage of creation, God designed and defined two crucial relationships to guide our

21

existence: an intended eternal relationship between mankind and him, and a marriage relationship between one man and one woman. As to the latter relationship, we are told that Eve was made from a rib extracted from Adam, and Eve was brought to Adam (Genesis 2:21-22).

The man said, "This is now bone of my bones and flesh of my flesh; she shall be called 'woman,' for she was taken out of man." That is why a man leaves his father and mother and is united to his wife, and they become one flesh. —— Genesis 2:23–24

Where Our Problems Began

The third chapter of Genesis jumps to the defining moment of our present existence and reveals our unfortunate natures.

> *Now the serpent was more crafty than any of the wild animals the Lord God had made. He said to the woman, "Did God really say, 'You must not eat from any tree in the garden'?"* — *Genesis 3:1*

The serpent enters the picture without any explanation of who or what he is. Revelation, the last book of the Bible, identifies the serpent as "that ancient serpent, who is the devil [Satan] (Revelation 20:2). There is a fair consensus that Satan, or the devil, was once an angel of the highest order in Heaven, who rebelled against God, perhaps thinking he was capable of being equal with God. He was cast out of Heaven to Earth, together with other disobedient angels, who were his followers. Angels are created beings who differ in abilities and natures from humans and by implication seem to predate the creation of mankind. We (mankind) were made a little lower than the angels (see Psalm 8:4–6).

It is important to note what the Bible says about Satan. Although God is all powerful and Satan is subject to God's authority, Satan holds a great deal of power over the events and lives of people on Earth. Why this is so remains one of the mysteries left unexplained in the Bible. Attempts to explain this would seem circumstantial at best.

Satan's authority on Earth is described in several verses. John 12:31 characterizes Satan as "the prince of this world [Earth]." More disturbingly, during one encounter, Satan tries to tempt Jesus to abandon God.

> *The devil led him up to a high place and showed him in an instant all the kingdoms of the world. And he said to him, "I will give you all their authority and splendor; it has been given to me, and I can give it to anyone I want to. If you worship me, it will all be yours." —* *Luke 4:5–7*

John tells us this:

> *The One who was born of God [Jesus] keeps [anyone born of God] safe, and the evil one cannot harm them.*

. . . The whole world is under the control of the evil one.
– 1 John 5:18–19

Satan's nature and methods are described in other verses.

He was a murderer from the beginning, not holding to the truth, for there is no truth in him. When he lies, he speaks his native language, for he is a liar and the father of lies. – John 8:44

Satan himself masquerades as an angel of light. – 2 Corinthians 11:14

Given our free will, the serpent cannot force us to do anything. But we are susceptible to his lies and distortions, which lead us astray and prompt us to satisfy our fallen natures, as opposed to doing what we know is right.

Satan attempts to confuse Eve with a lie, misstating what God has said.

The woman said to the serpent, "We may eat fruit from the trees in the garden, but God did say, 'You must not eat fruit from the tree that is in the middle of the garden, and you must not touch it, or you will die.'"—— Genesis 3:1–2

Eve is aware that there is a forbidden fruit, but she seems a little confused about the extent of the prohibition.

"You will not certainly die," the serpent said to the woman. "For God knows that when you eat from it your eyes will be opened, and you will be like God, knowing good and evil." — *Genesis 3:4–5*

The serpent follows with a half-truth combined with another lie, flavored by the implication that God is holding back something good from them. The serpent also claims that Eve "will be like God" if she eats the forbidden fruit. The latter thought, that we can be like God, is not only a complete lie, it is at the heart of a great portion of our troubles in life, not only personally but corporately as nations. The Bible warns us, there is none like God. We ignore this at our own peril.

Those who know the story know what comes next. Does Adam jump in and stop Eve from eating? Does Eve reject the serpent's temptation and follow God's command?

When the woman saw that the fruit of the tree was good for food and pleasing to the eye, and also desirable for gaining wisdom, she took some and ate it. She also gave some to her husband, who was with her, and he ate it. Then the eyes of both of them were opened, and they realized they were naked; so they sewed fig leaves together and made coverings for themselves. — Genesis 3:6–7

Three things motivated Eve to disobey God: the fruit looked good, it was edible, and best of all, it would make her like God. Some of the consequences to Adam and Eve were immediate, and some would come later. Unfortunately for mankind, the long-term consequences infected every generation of every human born from that time forward, through our present generation. Our sin natures are like a genetic defect carried by every person on Earth, a defect which we are powerless by ourselves to erase.

Adam and Eve immediately experienced shame. Before their disobedience, they were innocent children, heedless of being unclothed among all the unclothed creatures of creation. In an instant, they were transported from a perfect creation to one where, by their own hands, evil gained a foothold and began its reign. They knew they had done something very wrong. When God confronted them about their disobedience, their responses were classic. Thousands of years later, we still use the same kinds of excuses to justify our wrongful actions. Here's the dialogue—the same one repeated in households every day where children are caught doing something wrong, as well as in the halls of government when elected officials are caught in their misdeeds.

> *The man said, "The woman you put here with me— she gave me some fruit from the tree, and I ate it." Then the Lord God said to the woman, "What is this you have done?" The woman said, "The serpent deceived me, and I ate."* — Genesis 3:12–13

In other words, "It's all her/his/someone else's fault." The serpent apparently had nobody else to blame.

The long term consequences for the serpent and for Adam and Eve are then spelled out. The serpent is condemned to crawl on its belly and eat dust all its life. And of significance to us today, enmity is put between the serpent's offspring and the woman's.

> *[God said,] "I will put enmity between you and the woman, and between your offspring and hers; he will crush your head, and you will strike his heel."* — Genesis 3:15

We will circle back to the serpent and this verse later in this book.

This event thousands of years ago marks the beginning of the battle between good and evil, which

28

will continue until mankind's time on Earth ends in a colossal final war. We and the generations that follow are enmeshed in the ongoing battles leading up to that war. If you ever wondered why almost every fiction book or movie pits bad people against good, villains against heroes, there is the template. We mimic and reflect this age-old struggle of good versus evil in our entertainment and sporting events with little thought that there is a very real battle between good and evil in which we all participate without any choice. Adam's disobedience ensured that we can't sit on the sidelines as spectators. In fact, the idea that we are embroiled in such an invisible conflict makes us quite uncomfortable. It's easier to live in denial.

As for Eve, she and the generations of women to follow were made to suffer.

[God said to the woman], "I will make your pains in childbearing very severe; with painful labor you will give birth to children. Your desire will be for your husband, and he will rule over you." — Genesis 3:16

Adam's consequences to himself and all generations to follow are spelled out:

"Cursed is the ground because of you; through painful toil you will eat food from it all the days of your life. It

will produce thorns and thistles for you, and you will eat
the plants of the field. By the sweat of your brow you
will eat your food until you return to the ground."—
Genesis 3:17–19

Doesn't that sound like our days at work?
A final consequence is spelled out:

God said, "The man has now become like one of us,
knowing good and evil. He must not be allowed to reach
out his hand and take also from the tree of life and eat,
and live forever."— *Genesis 3:22 (emphasis added)*

God then banished Adam from the garden and
blocked his access to the tree of life.

This was the turning point in history, which has
defined mankind since the time of creation. With
one act of disobedience, the breaking of one simple
rule, we went from living in a garden paradise in an
innocent, childlike relationship with God our
heavenly Father to an existence filled with pain, toil,
evil, and death. Too harsh a result? Only if we try to
place ourselves on a plane equal to God. Isn't that
where Adam and Eve went wrong? And it appears,
Satan as well. They were all cast out of a paradise.

There is an issue presented by Genesis 2:15–17
which may trouble some of us, where Adam is
commanded not to eat the forbidden fruit and is told

the consequences. The NIV says "*when* you eat from it, you will surely die." That word *when* might be taken to signify that Adam's disobedience was an inevitable event and that God knew ahead of time that Adam would eventually disobey, which prompts the question of whether Adam truly had free will. The New Living Translation (NLT) reads "*if* you eat of its fruit, you are sure to die." The use of "if" implies free choice and an event that may or may not occur. This apparent conflict in translation can be reconciled by reference to the King James Version (KJV), which significantly predates the other versions. "But of the tree of the knowledge of good and evil, thou shalt not eat of it; for in the day that thou eatest thereof, thou shalt surely die." The KJV elegantly incorporates both "when" and "if," and its translation eliminates the apparent inconsistency and such questions which may follow.

Another subject of discussion is prompted by the phrase "you shall surely die." It does not say you shall physically die, although physical death is what we typically think of when we hear the word "die." But the fact that man was originally intended to live forever with God can be seen from the passage cutting off Adam from the tree of life, which would have enabled Adam to live forever. The tree of life

31

reappears in Revelation, the last book of the Bible, as perhaps the source of eternal life in Heaven.

In addition to eventual physical death, there is also a spiritual death that occurs when our relationship with God is broken. In the case of Adam and Eve, that spiritual death occurred immediately when they broke the only commandment God had given them, cutting off their connection to eternal life with God. Mankind has been spiritually dead, separated from God, since that time.

When we look around us at the killing, the wars, the hate, the death, the suffering and disease, and wonder why God permits this if he loves us, we should remember that life on Earth was never intended to be like this, and at one time long ago, it wasn't. While God may have the power to *stop* all of this, he didn't *start* it. Mankind did. Great numbers of mankind continue to exercise their free will by choosing evil over good, marching us down the same path. Our choices have consequences.

Let's look at some of the events in mankind's journey with God, which illustrate our poor choices that continue to separate us from God, while God patiently moves in the midst of our disobedience to reconcile us back to him.

The First Murder

Adam and Eve had two sons, Cain and Abel (along with other children). Cain became angry and jealous because God accepted an offering by Abel but rejected Cain's offering. Cain offered some of the fruits of the soil he worked, while Abel brought fat portions from some of the firstborn of his flock. Abel apparently offered the best and most valuable of the fruits of his labor, while Cain's offering was likely something of little value.

> *Cain was very angry, and his face was downcast. Then the Lord said to Cain, "Why are you angry? Why is your face downcast? If you do what is right, will you not be accepted? But if you do not do what is right, sin is crouching at your door; it desires to have you, but you must rule over it." — Genesis 4:5–7*

Cain had a choice: to admit he had done wrong and to change his behavior in the future, or to allow his rebellious anger to rule over him. So what choice did Cain make? Cain killed Abel. Has human nature changed since then? Do we continue to justify our actions and get angry over the consequences when we do something we know is wrong?

Two biblical principles that are foundational to understand our present circumstances and our path back to God are introduced in that passage: sin and sacrificial offering to God. Sin is simply introduced as not doing what is "right," without a full picture of how "right" is defined. Likewise, the practice of sacrificial offerings appears without any background reference. The original audience, those for whom Genesis was written, likely understood these concepts. For today's readers, their importance and explanation are fully developed subsequently throughout the Bible.

Defining sin is not an exacting matter. It has several facets. Some have defined three types of sin:

(1) *Original sin* (our inborn sin) started with and is characterized by Adam and Eve's rebellion and disobedience to God. This is the systemic sin that affects all of mankind—everyone. The Bible notes

that all have sinned and have fallen short of the glory of God—all of us (Romans 3:23).

(2) *Imputed sin* stems from violations of the law that God set forth to govern the lives of the nation of Israel. The Ten Commandments were supplemented with many other laws handed down to Israel. Disobedience again plays a part.

(3) *Personal sin* involves our everyday conduct: lying, stealing, malice, anger, sexual immorality, and other behaviors that violate his standards for our lives. Others note that sin is, or is characterized by, a fallen condition of the heart in relation to God, and is often a desire to obtain personal gain or some enticing reward without regard to the propriety of the means used or consequences to ourselves and others. Sin is not measured by how we stack up against other people's conduct. It is measured by the absolute holiness of God, who is without sin. Nothing tainted by sin can be tolerated in God's presence. The Bible tells us the wages of even one sin is death (Romans 6:23).

Offerings or sacrifices to God to atone for sins, both individual and corporate, were an integral and substantial part of the lives of the nation of Israel throughout its history. Sacrifice rituals were complex and elaborate. The sacrifices that God commanded the Israelites to follow are described at length in the Bible. Many involved the killing of animals and sacrificing them on an altar.

The necessity of a blood sacrifice was deeply ingrained in the life of Israel for all of its generations.

> *For the life of a creature is in the blood, and I have given it to you to make atonement for yourselves on the altar; it is the blood that makes atonement for one's life.*
> — *Leviticus 17:11*

> *Without the shedding of blood there is no forgiveness.*
> — *Hebrews 9:22*

With these principles in mind, let's return to the saga of humanity's journey with God after the downfall of Adam and Eve.

Mankind Begins Its Journey— And Gets Drowned

Following the creation of Adam and Eve, mankind began to increase in numbers but continued its pattern of evil behavior. Although those early people acknowledged God's existence, they chose a murderous and immoral lifestyle rather than living righteously. God gave mankind some 1,600 years to choose between righteous living and evil (see Genesis 5, which contains a chronology of the generations following Adam through Noah).

The Lord saw how great the wickedness of the human race had become on the earth, and that every inclination of the thoughts of the human heart was only evil all the time. The Lord regretted that he had made human beings on the earth, and his heart was deeply troubled. So the Lord said, "I will wipe from the face of the earth

the human race I have created—and with them the
animals, the birds and the creatures that move along the
ground—for I regret that I have made them." But Noah
found favor in the eyes of the Lord. — Genesis 6:5–8

What distinguished Noah? He was a righteous
man, blameless among the people of his time, and he
walked faithfully with God (Genesis 6:9).
Percentage-wise, we bombed out epically. Only
eight people, Noah and his family, were worth
saving.

God directed Noah to build an ark (boat) 450 feet
long, 75 feet wide, and 45 feet high, and to bring
aboard his wife, his three sons and their wives, and
two (one male, one female) of every animal and bird
species on Earth, together with food. Noah's three
sons were born when Noah was about 500 years old.
The flood occurred when Noah was 600 years old.
We aren't told how long it took to build the ark.
Various sources estimate fifty-five to seventy five
years. If God told any of us to build a boat
approaching the size of an ocean liner out of wood,
by hand, to escape an upcoming flood that had never
happened before, would we have faith to devote fifty
or more years to the task?

Once Noah, his family, and the animals were
aboard, God brought a flood that covered the earth,

killing everything except Noah and his family and the animals on the ark. Noah and the occupants of the ark were on board for about a year before the flood waters receded to the point that they could leave the ark and begin to repopulate the world as God had told them to do.

Were Noah's family and their descendants humbled into righteous living by knowing the devastating results of God's wrath against sinful mankind? Sadly, we know the answer.

God Starts Over

When Noah and his family disembarked from the ark, Noah built an altar and sacrificed a burnt offering of some of the animals and birds from the ark to God.

> [God] said in his heart: "Never again will I curse the ground because of humans, even though every inclination of the human heart is evil from childhood."
> — Genesis 8:21

God recognized the unfortunate condition of the human heart.

God told Noah and his sons to "be fruitful and increase in numbers and fill the earth" (Genesis 9:1). Noah's family began to repopulate the earth. The clans that devolved from them began to spread across the earth, having one language and a common speech

(Genesis 11:1). But after a time, a great mass of them gathered and settled on a plain in Shinar.

> *Then they said, "Come, let us build ourselves a city, with a tower that reaches to the heavens, so that we may make a name for ourselves; otherwise we will be scattered over the face of the whole earth." — Genesis 11:4*

Once again, mankind's pride dictated its actions, rather than God's commands. They ignored God's directive to spread throughout the earth and compounded their disobedience by purposing to build a tower to reach the heavens. Some analysts think the tower was intended to provide a way for a deity to come down to enter his temple to be worshipped—as if God required or would be pleased with their help in that regard. In any event, God viewed these actions as mankind's challenge to his sovereignty.

Another Reset

Once again, God found it necessary to intervene in man's affairs.

> *The Lord came down to see the city and the tower the people were building. The Lord said, "If as one people speaking the same language they have begun to do this, then nothing they plan to do will be impossible for them. Come, let us go down and confuse their language so they will not understand each other." So the Lord scattered them from there over all the earth, and they stopped building the city.* — *Genesis 11:5–8*

The phrase "nothing they plan to do will be impossible" is not considered literally. Rather, it may be interpreted to mean that collectively, large groups of people united around a common improper purpose have a great capacity for evil. We see this reflected today in the concentration of crime in large cities.

The Second Reboot—Abram

Two hundred ninety years after the flood, a man named Abram was born. (Note: the NIV study Bible consulted for this book does not attempt to assign a time or date before the birth of Jesus to the date of creation, the fall in the Garden of Eden, the flood, or the Tower of Babel. There is some scholarly debate as to the time of these events. The timelines prior to Abram's birth referenced above in this book were determined by following the dates given in the Bible for the successive births of Biblical characters following Adam and Eve and constitute the author's interpretation of those timespans. The study Bible ascribes the date of the birth of Abram as approximately 2,166 BC.)

The story of Abram, later renamed Abraham by God, and the generations of his descendants who became the nation of Israel, encompasses the remainder of the Old Testament. The next several pages of this book trace the birth and early life of that nation. Some may find this history slow-paced to read through, but it will reward the reader in understanding the roots of the ongoing Middle East crises, terrorism, and in seeing how God's hand has remained active in mankind over thousands of years. God does not abandon us despite our rebellious natures.

Abram embodies God's next attempt to reconcile fallen mankind. Abram was a man faithful to God. When Abram was seventy-five, God sent him away from his own country, his father's household, and his peoples to a land which God would later show him. This was unusual in that time and culture. People did not tend to move away from their families and people groups.

God promised Abram that he would make Abram into a great nation and that all the peoples on Earth would be blessed through him. Today's equivalent might be a command to quit our job, put all our belongings into a U-Haul, pack up our family and pets, and hit the road. God will tell us where to go after we're on the road. Would any of us have such faith in God that we would do that?

After Abram left his country, he lived in various locations, increasing in wealth, engaging in battle with hostile neighbors, all the while continuing to trust God. After a time, God appeared again to Abram in a vision, reminding him that he was his shield and very great reward. Abram appealed to God that the one great reward Abram and his wife Sarai lacked was children. God promised that Abram would have a son and that his offspring would be almost countless. God also foretold that Abram's descendants would be enslaved and mistreated in a foreign nation for four hundred years, but that God would punish that nation and Abram's descendants would leave with great possessions. Lastly, God promised that Abram's descendants would one day possess a great portion of the lands surrounding Abram.

Abram and his wife believed God—for a time. After about ten years had passed without Sarai conceiving, Sarai gave her maidservant, Hagar, to Abram to bear a child (this was a custom of the day, although it is one of those practices we can't grasp today). Sarai and Abram were not content to allow God to fulfill his promise at the time God saw fit, and they decided to take matters into their own hands.

Ishmael and Isaac—The Birth of the Arabs and Israelites

When Hagar became pregnant, she chided Sarai, and hostility developed between them. Hagar fled to the wilderness. In her misery, God appeared to her.

"You will give birth to a son. You shall name him Ishmael, for the Lord has heard of your misery. He will be a wild donkey of a man; his hand will be against everyone and everyone's hand against him, and he will live in hostility toward all his brothers."— Genesis 16:11–12

Hagar returned to Abram's household and gave birth to Ishmael when Abram was 86.

When Abram was 99, God appeared to him again and repeated his earlier promise that Abram and Sarai would have a son together, saying the son is to be named Isaac. God established an everlasting covenant between himself and Abram's descendants born of Sarai, from whom would come many nations and kings. Abram and Sarai were renamed Abraham and Sarah. Abraham asked God for a blessing for Ishmael as well, and God granted that Ishmael would have numerous descendants and would be the father of twelve rulers. However, God made it clear that his covenant would be established with Isaac.

Isaac was born at the time God said he would be born, when Abraham was 100 years old. When Isaac was two or three years old, the tensions between Sarah and Hagar erupted again. Hagar and Ishmael were cast out of Abraham's household when Ishmael was about fifteen. However, God kept his promise, and Hagar and Ishmael were cared for. Ishmael eventually fathered twelve sons, who became the rulers of twelve tribes. The tribes "lived in hostility toward all of the tribes related to them" (Genesis 25:18).

Abraham thus became the father of the nation of Israel, the Jewish peoples who have existed as the descendants of Abraham and a separate people group from all others since that time. They will be present on Earth through the end of times. It is widely considered that Ishmael's descendants are the Arabs of today, who have warred with Israel since those early times. That conflict intensified with the establishment of Islam as a predominant religion in the Middle East about 1,400 years ago. God's pronouncement that Ishmael's descendants would have their hand against brother Isaac's has borne bitter fruit, as seen in the Islamic terrorist attacks that have increased dramatically since the 1970s.

We see clearly throughout history the widespread and often catastrophic results that occur when individuals or nations choose to ignore God's direction and take matters into their own hands.

The disobedience of Adam and Eve, and Abraham and Sarah's refusal to wait on God's timing for her to bear a child, have had devastating consequences for mankind, which persist yet today.

Captivity in Egypt

The early generations of Israelites migrated to Egypt, the dominant regional power, to escape a famine. After a period of peaceful coexistence, the Egyptians became alarmed at the rapid population growth of the Israelites. In fear of being overtaken in numbers and power by the Israelites, Egypt's military subdued Israel and subjugated its people to slavery.

After four hundred years of brutal slavery, the Israelites cried out to God to free them from captivity. God heard their cry and chose a man named Moses to lead the Israelites out of Egypt. Moses approached Egypt's leader, Pharaoh, with a demand to free the Israelites. Pharaoh was warned that refusal would bring suffering upon Egypt by the hand of the God of Israel. Pharaoh refused, and was confronted by a series of ten progressively worsening plagues. Crops were devoured by locusts; festering

50

boils erupted on people and animals; hail rained down, killing people and animals; insects plagued the land. After each plague, Moses repeated his demand, and was refused.

The last plague took the lives of the firstborn sons of all the Egyptians, including Pharaoh's own son. Before the plague arrived, God instructed the Israelites to smear the blood of lambs over the door frames of their homes. The plague passed over the homes of the Israelites, and their children were spared. This event was named the Passover, and it is still celebrated by Jewish people today as one of their religious holidays.

After this plague, Pharaoh relented and allowed the Israelites to depart from Egypt. On their way out, the Israelites were showered with gold, silver, and clothing by the Egyptians. All this took place just as God had foretold Abraham it would, seven hundred years earlier.

Moving Day

There are differences of opinion as to the number of Israelites who left Egypt. The Bible says there were about "600,000 men on foot, besides women and children" (Exodus 12:37). Adding women and children, estimates conclude that it was well over one million, plus the livestock.

After the Israelites left, they came upon the Red Sea. Pharaoh was having second thoughts about letting his entire free labor force leave and sent his army and charioteers after the Israelites to bring them back. Trapped between Pharaoh's armies and the Red Sea, the Israelites railed against Moses, sure that they would be killed. They did not yet have faith in God that he would deliver them. Moses prayed to God and was told to stretch his staff over the sea. God parted the Red Sea allowing the Israelites to cross over. Once they were ashore on the other side,

God collapsed the waters over the pursuing army, drowning the Egyptians.

The Israelites embarked into the desert and wandered there for a time. Before long, the people began to grumble against Moses and his brother, Aaron, who were leading the people under God's direction, about the lack of food and water. God provided water and a form of bread called *manna*, which fell from the skies. God also provided quail.

Moses Goes to School

Three months after leaving Egypt, the Israelites came to the Sinai Desert, encamping there after defeating the army of the Amalekites, with God's power bringing victory. Moses was summoned by God to Mount Sinai, where God began to communicate with Moses. The instructions given through Moses to Israel would form the basis of the extensive code of conduct to govern the entire life practices of the nation of Israel, including worship activities, from that time forward.

God's first instructions to Moses were to tell the Israelites:

> *"You yourselves have seen what I did to Egypt, and how I carried you on eagles' wings and brought you to myself. Now if you obey me fully and keep my covenant, then out of all nations you will be my treasured possession. Although the whole earth is mine, you will be*

for me a kingdom of priests and a holy nation."—
Exodus 19:4–6

God set Israel apart as his chosen people. As God had promised Abraham, God would continue to focus his blessings upon Israel, Abraham's descendants. But importantly, Israel was required to obey God and keep his covenant in order to continue to receive God's blessing. The rest of mankind was left to its own devices.

After that, God showed his presence to the Israelites:

> *There was thunder and lightning, with a thick cloud over the mountain, and a very loud trumpet blast. Everyone in the camp trembled. Then Moses led the people out of the camp to meet with God, and they stood at the foot of the mountain. Mount Sinai was covered with smoke, because the Lord descended on it in fire. The smoke billowed up from it like smoke from a furnace, and the whole mountain trembled violently. . . . The sound of the trumpet grew louder and louder. — Exodus 19:16–19*

> *When the people saw the thunder and lightning and heard the trumpet and saw the mountain in smoke, they trembled with fear. — Exodus 20:18*

The Israelites were ordered to stay off the mountain, as it was holy ground. They were happy to comply after seeing the fearsome demonstration of God's power. Moses embarked upon several trips up the mountain to receive God's instructions. Moses received the Ten Commandments to be followed by Israel and duly instructed the Israelites to follow them: The first two are: you shall have no other gods before me and (paraphrased) you shall not make unto me any graven image (a man-made idol of wood, gold, silver). Idol worship and polytheism (the worship of multiple gods) were rampant among the nations surrounding the Israelites.

One of Moses' excursions up the mountain kept him away from the encampment forty days.

When the people saw that Moses was so long in coming down from the mountain, they gathered around Aaron and said, "Come, make us gods who will go before us. As for this fellow Moses who brought us up out of Egypt, we don't know what has happened to him."—Exodus 32:1

Let this sink in: here are a people who have just experienced the following things from God, who has commanded them, you shall have no other gods before me and you shall not make idols to worship:

- God brought ten plagues on Egypt, none of which harmed the Israelites.

- God spared their children from the final death plague when they followed God's command to mark their door frames with blood.

- God brought over one million of them out of 400 years of captivity, parting the seas to allow them to escape the pursuing Egyptian army.

- God produced water and food for them in a desert that had neither, gave them a military victory over an attacking foe, and displayed his awesome might over Mount Sinai such that the people were afraid to approach the mountain out of fear of God.

It took only forty days of Moses' absence for the Israelites to abandon God after all they had just experienced.

Aaron, Moses brother, who had been part of the way up the mountain to accompany Moses on his way to meet with God, had the people bring him their gold earrings.

He took what they handed him and made it into an idol cast in the shape of a calf, fashioning it with a tool. Then they said, "These are your gods, Israel, who brought you up out of Egypt." — Exodus 32:4

Aaron built an altar in front of the calf and called for a festival. The next day, the people sacrificed burnt offerings and presented fellowship offerings. They then sat down to eat and drink, and got up to indulge in revelry.

> *The Lord said to Moses, "Go down, because your people, whom you brought up out of Egypt, have become corrupt. They have been quick to turn away from what I commanded them."— Exodus 32:7–8*

God then described to Moses exactly what the people had done.

> *"They are a stiff-necked people. Now leave me alone so that my anger may burn against them and that I may destroy them. Then I will make you into a great nation." — Exodus 32:9–10*

Moses pleaded with God to relent from destroying the people, and God relented. Moses returned to the camp and saw the golden calf idol and the people running wild. He confronted Aaron, who confessed to what he had done.

> *"Do not be angry, my lord," Aaron answered. "You know how prone these people are to evil." — Exodus 32:22*

In other words, "It's all their fault." Sound familiar?

Moses called out to the camp for whoever was for the Lord to come to him. The Levites came forward. Moses told them that God had directed that they take swords.

> "Go back and forth through the camp from one end to the other, each killing his brother and friend and neighbor." — Exodus 32:27

The Levites did as commanded. About three thousand people died.

Moses returned to Mount Sinai to seek forgiveness for the people's sins. The Lord made it clear that he had remained angry with the people and that, in his time, he would punish them for their sins. The people were struck with a plague because of what they had done with the golden calf.

Moses continued to commune with God. At one point, he asked that God reveal his glory to him. The Lord allowed Moses a glimpse of his glory.

> And he passed in front of Moses, proclaiming, "The Lord, the Lord, the compassionate and gracious God, slow to anger, abounding in love and faithfulness, maintaining love to thousands, and forgiving wickedness, rebellion and sin. Yet he does not leave the

guilty unpunished; he punishes the children and their
children for the sin of the parents to the third and fourth
generation."— Exodus 34:6–7

By this statement the Lord himself revealed many
of his attributes to us. He was well aware of the
rebellious natures of the people and warned that
their sin would have long-lasting consequences.

The Next Thousand Years

The nation of Israel eventually broke camp and moved onward. Its journey and history after the events described in Exodus, as chronicled in the Bible, span another thousand years. The Exodus from Egypt is dated at about 1,446 BC. The last book of the Old Testament, Malachi, is dated about 430 BC. During the interim period between the book of Exodus and the book of Malachi, we see repeated cycles of the Israelites' obedience and worship of God and the blessings such as peace, military success, and prosperity that come with obedience—followed by periods of disobedience and lack of trust and proper worship of God, which resulted in punishment of Israel by military defeats in numerous wars and being taken into captivity as a nation. This thousand-year segment of Israel's history takes about one thousand pages in the Bible.

We could study many more examples of mankind's and Israel's relationship with God during this period, but they would illustrate the same themes. God's intent for Israel was to remain set apart from other nations as God's chosen people by adherence to the laws and practices commanded by God, by absolute trust in God for protection and sustenance, the worship of God only, and cultural separation from other nations. In contrast to Israel, other nations practiced rituals abhorrent to God, such as child sacrifice, idol worship, and prostitution as part of their religious rites. Israelites were forbidden from marrying men and women of the other cultures and intermingling cultural practices. During its times of obedience, Israel recorded astonishing military victories over its foes, against seemingly impossible odds. The other nations saw this and realized that the one true God of Israel was indeed superior to the many gods and idols they worshipped. When Israel drifted apart from God and intermingled and intermarried with other cultures, or simply abandoned its proper trust and worship of God, there was always a price to pay.

There are none so blind as those who refuse to see.

Prophets and Prophesies

From its earliest times, God chose various Israelite men of great faith as prophets to bring God's messages, warning the people of impending judgment when they fell into disobedience, and foretelling future events. God never punished the Israelites for their sins without first giving them more than ample time to repent and change their ways. Seventeen books of the Old Testament are named after prophets, showing how frequently Israel strayed so far that God found it necessary to send prophets.

In addition to their warnings, the prophets announced the coming one day of a Messiah who would lead Israel to peace and righteousness and return it to superiority and prominence over the other nations. The people had been conquered and ruled by other nations so often that the people longed for the appearance of the Messiah, whom they likely believed would be a military leader.

Malachi is the last prophet mentioned in the Bible. In Malachi 1, we find an exchange between the Lord and the people of Israel, in the form of a dialogue between Malachi and the priests (chosen officials since the time of Exodus to carry out the sacrifices and rituals in the temple to honor God and atone for the sins of the people).

God says to the people, "Where is the respect due to me? You priests show contempt for my name."

The priests ask, "How have we showed contempt for you and defiled you?"

God answers, "By offering defiled food on my altar. When you offer blind, lame, or diseased animals."

Does this sound familiar? Recall that Cain's offering was displeasing to God, likely for the same reasons. People's natures and attitudes toward God have not improved. Have they gotten any better since the beginning of mankind? Does our society today show respect for God or contempt?

The vast and remarkable story of Israel in the Old Testament parallels mankind's path to the present time. Mankind as a whole has continued to distinguish itself with murder, wars, and idol worship, and a resolute desire to live in disrespect to God.

A period of about four-hundred years elapses from the last book of the Old Testament to the first book of the New Testament, Matthew. As we leave the Old Testament, we see that Israel has chosen for two-thousand years to repeatedly stray from God in disobedience. The remainder of mankind has continued its pagan practices. Sin seems to have firm control of the world.

The New Testament—God's Final Reboot

The New Testament introduces a revolutionary shift in God's relationship with his people. For centuries, the law has been the sole source of Israel's pathway to God. But the law is about to become secondary, and God's promise of blessing through Abraham will expand from the nation of Israel to include all mankind.

Two thousand years ago, the nation of Israel was subjected to the rule of the Roman empire. Rome held a firm grip on its vast conquered territory, enforced by its military. Israel was hard-wired in its religious structure and practices. The Roman government allowed some measure of religious freedom to the Israelites to prevent unrest, so long as there was no disruption of civil order or challenge to the authority of Rome. The law handed down to Moses had grown so that most elements of daily life were subject to some facet of the law. The arbiters of the law were religious officials, including priests, teachers of the law, and elders. These men dressed in finery, were given deference and honor, and enjoyed being celebrities in the community. Their strict and rigid adherence to the law made them, in their own eyes, superior to the average citizens and closer to God. They presided over their own religious courts to enforce the law of Israel, which was often harsh. A woman caught in adultery was to be stoned to death. Worship took place at a temple, an ornate physical structure where sacrifices were made to God.

The first temple was commissioned by God at the time of Exodus and decreed to remain a permanent fixture in Israel's worship. It had a very specific design directed by God, with outer and inner courtyards and rooms. The innermost room where God's presence would appear was accessible only to the priests, who were the only ones permitted to perform the high ceremonies and sacrifices required by the law. The average citizens were barred from the inner chambers.

The necessity of shedding blood in sacrifice to atone for sin was a practice firmly embedded in

Israel's culture. God's absolute holiness cannot tolerate the presence of sin. The wages of sin is death, and sin requires payment through the sacrificial shedding of blood.

In this cultural and historic setting, perhaps the most important event in history occurs: the first Christmas, the birth of Jesus Christ, a descendant of Abraham. The Christmas story is familiar to many. A virgin named Mary was pledged to be married to a man named Joseph. Before they came together, Mary was visited by the Holy Spirit of God and conceived a child, who was to be called Jesus. Joseph, who was considering divorce because of Mary's pregnancy, was visited by an angel of the Lord who told him that the child was conceived of the Holy Spirit and that the child would save his people from their sin. Joseph honored what the angel said and did not divorce Mary. He took her to be his wife. All this took place to fulfill what the Lord had said through the prophet Isaiah some seven hundred years earlier:

> *The virgin will conceive and give birth to a son, and will call him Immanuel. — Isaiah 7:14*

Isaiah also proclaimed this prophecy regarding Jesus birth:

For to us a child is born, to us a son is given, and the government will be on his shoulders. And he will be called Wonderful Counselor, Mighty God, Everlasting Father, Prince of Peace. Of the greatness of his government and peace there will be no end. He will reign on David's throne and over his kingdom, establishing and upholding it with justice and righteousness from that time on and forever. The zeal of the Lord Almighty will accomplish this. — Isaiah 9:6–7

Jesus was born in Bethlehem, fulfilling these and other prophecies.

Here is a mystery that we cannot grasp. Jesus was fully God and fully human at the same time. In fact, God exists in three forms: God the Father, God the Son (Jesus), and God the Holy Spirit. Yet he is One God. There are things about God which we will never understand. We must simply accept them. Each time you think about God, think back to his attributes listed by Tozer. Indeed, God can take any form or forms he chooses. If this concept is troubling, here is an analogy that might help: if you put a block of ice in a pan and set the pan on a stove, eventually as the ice melts and boils away, the same material will be simultaneously ice, water, and steam. This is a weak analogy to a divine concept, but perhaps makes it easier to picture.

Jesus was born in a humble stable, hardly what one would expect for the birth of a king. When he was about thirty, Jesus began a three-year ministry, proclaiming himself as the long-awaited Messiah whose coming was foretold by the Old Testament prophets. He urged the people to follow him. He chose twelve disciples to be his closest companions and followers and travelled from place to place with them. Jesus preached the new covenant of redemption through faith in him, instructed people in godly living, and performed many spectacular miracles, healing the sick, lame, and blind, even raising a man named Lazarus from the dead. His message was one of love, forgiveness, and righteousness. He urged people to forgive their enemies, not to seek vengeance.

Jesus interacted with sinners such as tax collectors and prostitutes, and with the lower classes of society—all of whom were shunned by the Jewish priests and religious leaders. Jesus' behavior raised the indignation of the religious leaders. He proclaimed himself to be one with God.

"I and the Father are one." — *John 10:30*

Perhaps his most revolutionary and important proclamation was this:

> *"I am the way and the truth and the life. No one comes to the Father except through me."* — *John 14:6*

No longer was the way to God through strict obedience to the law, as preached by the religious leaders. Belief in Jesus was the new covenant between God and man, replacing the law as the path to salvation. The religious leaders were essentially out of a job.

One of the most familiar Bible passages summarizes why God sent Jesus into the world:

> *For God so loved the world that he gave his one and only Son, that whoever believes in him shall not perish but have eternal life. For God did not send his Son into the world to condemn the world, but to save the world through him.* — *John 3:16–17*

God realizes that we are incapable of obedient and righteous living, of adhering to any divine law without falling and stumbling. Our inherited sin natures, combined with the influence of the devil, lead us astray continually. Out of his mercy and grace, God sent Jesus to become a substitute sacrifice for all mankind, to reconcile us and redeem us from our sin. This he did at a time when we were his enemies, deserving only condemnation.

> *As for you [those who have turned to Jesus], you were dead in your transgressions and sins, in which you used to live when you followed the ways of this world and of the ruler of the kingdom of the air [Satan], the spirit who is now at work in those who are disobedient. All of us also lived among them at one time, gratifying the cravings of our flesh and following its desires and thoughts. Like the rest, we were by nature deserving of wrath. But because of his great love for us, God, who is rich in mercy, made us alive with Christ even when we were dead in transgressions. . . . For it is by grace you have been saved, through faith—and this is not from yourselves, it is the gift of God—not by works, so that no one can boast.* — Ephesians 2:1–9

The priests and religious leaders were enraged by Jesus' messages and were greatly troubled by the growing large numbers of his followers. If this were not enough, Jesus shamed the religious leaders publicly for their hard hearts and lack of love and compassion. They were blind to who he was and plotted to kill him. Eventually they succeeded in having him arrested and convicted on false charges in a succession of unlawful trials. Jesus was publically flogged (whipped) on his back until his flesh was raw. Near death from that, he was forced to carry the crossbar of a heavy wooden cross through the streets up to a hill where he was nailed to the cross, through his hands and feet, and left to hang there until he died a slow and agonizing death. Just before he died, Jesus asked the most profound *WHY?* that will be ever be uttered in mankind's history:

About three in the afternoon Jesus cried out in a loud voice, . . . "My God, my God, why have you forsaken me?"— Matthew 27:46

At that time, Jesus took on the entire sin of mankind, and his intimate connection with God was temporarily broken. All of our "whys" about our own sufferings pale in comparison.

How could anything good come out of the most unjust execution in history? The death of the one man in all history—past, present, and future—who was sinless, without guilt or shame of any kind, the one man who had lived in perfect obedience to God, to the point of dying on the cross.

The answer is this: the sin of mankind requires payment. The wages of sin is death. Jesus paid the price for the sin of all mankind through his blood shed for us through his death on the cross so we may have eternal life when we accept him as our Lord and Savior. This is a gift from God. Nothing we can ever do or say, no amount of good works, will qualify us to spend eternity in Heaven. Jesus is our one path and our one hope. Our human depravity was so great that it required the sacrifice of the very Son of God, who was blameless and sinless, to pay our debt for our sin. This is how much God loves us—that he would send his only Son to die for us so we might have eternal life with God, just as God intended from the beginning of time.

Jesus' body was placed in a tomb, with a stone rolled over the front to prevent his body from being removed. Three days later, he arose from that grave. He conquered death for us. Over the next forty or so days, Jesus appeared to some five hundred people, including his closest followers, eleven disciples. (There were originally twelve; one of the twelve, Judas Iscariot, betrayed him, leading to his arrest and death. Judas committed suicide after that.)

After his resurrection and appearance, Jesus was taken up into Heaven in full view of some of his disciples, where he sits today at God's right hand. Before he departed Earth, Jesus commissioned his disciples to spread the good news that salvation has come through Jesus' death and resurrection. From that handful of men, the news spread and continues to be spread throughout the world today.

After his death and resurrection, the message of Jesus was first meant for, and carried to, the people of Israel. The Israelites were ingrained with the concept of the necessity of a blood sacrifice for the payment of sin, and they should have understood that Jesus' sacrifice was meant to pay for all their sins. It superseded the need for any further animal sacrifices. But the Israelites, who were originally God's chosen people, were resistant to this truth, and most would not accept it. In accordance with his plan, God in his great mercy commissioned apostles to spread the message to the gentiles (non-Jews) as well, and the followers of this new faith grew by the thousands.

Aside from a small number, the Jewish people of today continue to follow the law rather than Jesus. They do not recognize or acknowledge him as the promised Messiah. While this causes friction between Jews and Christians, this should not be so. God loves both groups, and we are commanded to love one another. Salvation through Jesus was made known and available to everyone universally, and it remains so today. God's promise to Abraham over two-thousand years before Jesus' birth is fulfilled in Jesus.

Another two thousand years have passed since Jesus came. Mankind has been at war somewhere on Earth almost continually since that time. Our natures have not changed since the time humans were first created. In 1948, the nation of Israel finally achieved statehood, with its own physical geographic territory and boundaries. It is surrounded by hostile nations and continual military threats and attacks. Some of its enemies have threatened to wipe it from the face of the earth. Yet for some four thousand years, the Jewish people have continued to exist, despite overwhelming odds, and despite being at war, not just recently but on and off during the entire time of their existence since Abraham. Are these facts alone sufficient to prove the existence of God? Some think so.

Another Enemy that Isn't Us

In addition to our sinful natures, another force has been at work since Adam and Eve to disrupt God's creation and promote mankind's downfall. Remember the serpent? The serpent is the embodiment of Satan, who has continued since the time of Adam and Eve to wage war against God and his creation. He, his weapons, and his minions are invisible. The battleground is our minds and our thoughts, and his weapons are lies, distortions, and temptations.

We find ourselves in the midst of a culture that has degenerated to the point where rational discussion of differences is no longer possible. Political and social discourse has fallen to the level of hate-filled personal attacks and vicious lies. Who is the master of lies? What is the opposite of love? Of course, it is hate. Once a heart is filled with hate, it is easy to manipulate with lies and distortions that feed the hate. Hate itself can be birthed and implanted by lies. If we think the enemy is some foreign country or some politician or particular group, the true enemy has us right where he wants us, deceived and fighting one another. Is there a defense against such lies?

An apostle (follower of Jesus) named Paul wrote most of the books of the New Testament. Here is how he describes the battlefield:

Put on the full armor of God, so that you can take your stand against the devil's schemes. For our struggle is not against flesh and blood, but against the rulers, against the authorities, against the powers of this dark world and against the spiritual forces of evil in the heavenly realms. — Ephesians 6:11

Too much for us to swallow? A bunch of fairy tales? Or the truth? Germs and air are invisible, yet they exist. If we decide to disbelieve this, we are easy prey for our enemy. The Bible tells us, the truth shall set us free. Do we want to be free?

Is Satan the cause of evil, or merely the catalyst to push evil human inclinations into action? Or perhaps some of both. Recall God's pronouncement after the flood.

Every inclination of the human heart is evil from childhood. — Genesis 8:21

When Cain killed Abel, we find no mention of the serpent's prompting, although God warns Cain that if he does not do right, sin is crouching at his door. The early Israelites seemed to need no prompting to turn from God and worship the golden calf.

These incidents perhaps indicate that it is our fallen hearts that are the core of the problem. But given this condition, we are easy victims of Satan without the protection of God's "armor." Some of Satan's lies come from the lips of others. Some appear as thoughts in our minds. Have you ever heard anyone say the following to you? Or have you thought these things?

- "You'll never amount to anything. You're a loser."
- "God could never love you. Look at all the bad stuff you've done."
- "I'll never have any fun if I become a Christian. I'll have to give up _____" (booze, drugs, sex—fill in the blank).
- "You need to get even with that guy who _____" (insulted you, cut you off in traffic, etc).

79

- "Evolution and science explain everything. There's no such thing as God."
- "Bad things happen to good people. No sense in believing in God."
- "You'll never be able to shake your addiction. Might as well give in to it and enjoy the high."
- "I'm a good person, and I go to church. I know I'll get into Heaven."

God's armor is available, but not to everyone. The protection is available to those who believe in Jesus Christ as their Lord and Savior. Without it, everyone is vulnerable to Satan's influence.

A suit of armor consists of several parts. The first piece of God's armor is the shield of faith in Jesus. The belt of truth, the breastplate of righteousness, the feet fitted with the gospel peace, the helmet of salvation, and the sword of the Holy Spirit complete the suit of armor (see Ephesians 6:13-19). But it is necessary for us to learn how to use that armor in order for it to be effective. The process is not automatic nor necessarily intuitive. We must actively don the armor every day.

The first step is simple. Invite Jesus into your life.

If you declare with your mouth, "Jesus is Lord," and believe in your heart that God raised him from the dead,

you will be saved. For it is with your heart that you
believe and are justified, and it is with your mouth that
you profess your faith and are saved. As Scripture says,
"Anyone who believes in him will never be put to shame."
— *Romans 10:9*

That declaration must include our acknowledgement that we are sinners in need of God's grace.

The second step, defeating the schemes of the devil, activating the armor of God, requires some participation on our part. Living rightly in obedience to the Lord, maintaining faith, prayer, and knowing the word of God in the Bible (the truth) all play a role.

Faith in Jesus is our individual answer to many of our struggles in the world, but unless the entire world were to accept God's gift, the rest of mankind will continue down its destructive path.

In Genesis, God foretold that the serpent's head will be crushed. This occurred when Jesus conquered death and sin on the cross for us. Satan and sin are defeated and can no longer control those who accept Jesus as their Lord and Savior. We are still susceptible to the tendency to sin and to the influence of the devil, but we can overcome this. It can no longer control us—unless we allow it to.

81

Our Latest Report Card

Terrorism, school shootings, war, hatred that's tearing our country and the world apart, cancer, poverty—maybe we're not doing too well. It doesn't help that God has been banned from our public schools, nor that we are allowing God's enemies to erase every mention of faith from the public sector. As a country and a world, we're collectively no better off than we were thousands of years ago.

Some people refuse to accept the existence of the devil. But much of what we witness today can only be the result of pure evil. Is there any coherent explanation of random massacres and school shootings other than evil at work? How about believing there is a God who will really be happy with us if we slaughter and behead certain other people?

82

But if God is all powerful and loves us, how come he doesn't stop all the bad stuff? We may never have a satisfactory answer to that. Or maybe that's not the right question. We know that (1) we are being allowed to suffer the consequences of our own bad choices despite thousands of years of opportunity to do what we know is right, and (2) we are pushovers for the enemy to activate our inherent sin natures. What would it look like if God did what we wish for, right now?

In order to stop all the "bad" stuff people are doing, God would have to change the millions of us who are currently living and everyone to be born in the future by taking our free will away and replacing it with a programmed mindset that somehow prevents us from doing anything bad, and instead living in strict obedience to a predetermined set of rules. But we can't even agree among ourselves what's bad and good, beyond perhaps murder and violent crimes. Sexual activites? Social injustice? Can we even agree whether our free will is a blessing or a curse? Good luck finding consensus.

God could also force us to return his love for us by loving him. What kind of life would that be? What kind of love would forced love be? What is the value of any relationship that is forced rather than voluntary, genuine, and responsive? Is it loving to change us from people with free will to a bunch of controlled people? Maybe we're asking the wrong question.

The Real Question—And the Answer

Our question really is this: why doesn't God stop the bad stuff *right now!* in our lifetime so we who are present don't have to deal with it anymore? Or as a corollary, why hasn't God done so already? But we already have the answer, given in the book of Revelation. God is, in fact, going to stop all the bad stuff. He is just not going to do it on our timetable. He wants as many as possible to come to him before the end times.

> *[God] is patient with you, not wanting anyone to perish, but everyone to come to repentance.* — *2 Peter 3:9*

Individually, we have the invitation right now to accept Jesus as our Lord and Savior. That won't stop all the bad that's happening in the world, and it doesn't guarantee us insulation from bad things that might happen to us. It does bring about a peace and joy while we finish our time on Earth. It does prompt us to change our focus on life and to examine our own misguided ways. And it brings the assurance that death is not the end. We will spend eternity with God in Heaven. God loved us enough to die for us, but it seems we always want more.

We know from the Bible that someday Jesus will return to Earth, and mankind will be judged and separated into two groups: those who have accepted Jesus and those who have not. The latter group, together with Satan and his followers, will spend eternity in Hell, a place of fire and torment. Those who choose Jesus will spend eternity in Heaven with God.

> *[God] will wipe every tear from their eyes. There will be no more death' or mourning or crying or pain, for the old order of things has passed away.* — Revelation 21:4

The end of times when this occurs will come with a colossal battle that centers around Jerusalem. Why is Israel always in the news? Jerusalem has always been ground zero for the struggle between God's forces of good and Satan's forces of evil. Today it is at the intersection of Judaism, Islam, and Christianity, a city of central importance to all three faiths and the subject of bitter divisions between them over who has the right to claim the city as theirs. The book of Revelation describes the final battle and the ultimate triumph of God over evil and gives us a beautiful depiction of Heaven and a frightening glimpse of Hell.

Our Inescapable Choice

When it comes to Jesus, there is no option to remain neutral. We can't abstain from voting. Everyone must choose to either accept or reject him.

Jesus said, "Whoever is not with me is against me" (Matthew 2:30; Luke 11:23). God is not going to change the world on our timetable, but he is going to do it in his own time. Jesus could return tomorrow, or a thousand years from now. Over the years various people have claimed to predict the day. So far they are batting zero.

> *But about that day or hour no one knows, not even the angels in Heaven, nor the Son, but only the Father.* — *Matthew 24:36*

But we ought to be ready.

> *For you know very well that the day of the Lord will come like a thief in the night.* — *1 Thessalonians 5:2*

That day will come unexpectedly, without warning.

If you would like to accept Jesus as your Lord and Savior, a simple prayer like this coming from your heart is all that is needed:

Lord Jesus, I want you to come into my life. Thank you for dying on the cross for my sins. I receive you as my Lord and Savior. Thank you for forgiving my sins and giving me eternal life. Please make me the kind of person you want me to be.

According to the Bible, God gave us a perfect world at the time of creation. With Satan's help, we have managed to ruin it. God has allowed us the consequences of our bad choices. God will restore his perfect creation. All those who have accepted Jesus as their Lord and Savior can overcome the influence of the devil, and will spend eternity in Heaven. Those who reject God's gift will spend eternity in Hell.

Conclusion

Life would be simpler if there was a book that answered all our questions. The Bible doesn't answer *all* of them, but it gives us enough information to understand a great deal about how and why we are where we are today, individually and as a world. And it tells us where we can find rest for our souls and hope for our futures in this troubled world. Is it true? We must each decide.

Faith is a choice.

Life is short. Eternity is not.

About the Author

James Downey is a retired attorney, an army veteran, and a student of comparative religion. He is also the author of *The Evolution of Jihad*, written under the pen name H. Davidson (available from Amazon), which explores the roots of Islam and how the search for the One True God of Abraham 1,400 years ago led to the terrorism we face today.

Made in the USA
Monee, IL
10 June 2023